WESTMINSTER PUBLIC LIBRARY

3 8020 01145 6133

CH
SO-AKZ-918

Dottie Lamm
A Friend to Families

Westminster Public Library
3705 W 112th Avenue
Westminster, CO 80031
westminsterlibrary.org

DISCARD

Dottie Lamm
A Friend to Families

A NOW YOU  KNOW BIO

Emily B. Warner

Filter Press, LLC
Palmer Lake, Colorado

To Abbey, Austin, Kaitlyn, Curtis, Gillian, and Matthew, who have learned the joy of discovery through the world of books.

Dottie Lamm: A Friend to Families
A Now You Know Bio
Number 8 in the Now You Know series

Copyright © 2007 Emily B. Warner
ISBN: 978-086541-085-5
Library of Congress Control Number: 2007934255

All rights reserved. No part of this publication may be reproduced or transmitted in any form or by any means, electronic or mechanical, including photocopy, recording, or any information storage and retrieval system, without permission in writing from the publisher. Contact Filter Press, LLC at 888.570.2663.

Filter Press, LLC, P.O. Box 95, Palmer Lake, Colorado.
www.filterpressbooks.com

Printed in the United States of America

Contents

1 Big House, Small Family

Dorothy Vennard Lamm approached the Boettcher Mansion in Denver, Colorado, with much **apprehension**. She took each step slowly, trying to enjoy the moment, but feeling a concern that she could hardly understand. Her husband, Richard Lamm, walked with their seven-year-old son, Scott, close by his side. Dottie—as she had been called since childhood—and daughter Heather, four years old, dropped a little behind to get a better look at the twenty-seven-room mansion that they would call their home for at least the next four years. Richard had been elected governor, and this was the family's first look at the Governor's Mansion since his election.

Dottie had helped her husband campaign for governor during 1973 and 1974. They had both worked tirelessly and were successful. Now on January 28, 1975,

Governor Dick Lamm took on his new job. It was exciting to think that they had worked so hard and had accomplished such a high goal. Why, then, did Dottie feel so **reluctant** to walk right up to that door and go in? Years later, Dottie said, "I suddenly realized I could be a powerful **influence** for women and children and the issues that are important to them, but I wasn't sure how well I would do."

The new first lady of Colorado moved inside the entrance, as curiosity won over her doubts about living in such a fine place. Dottie and Heather gazed down the long hallway to the splendid Palm Room far ahead. They passed beautiful antique furniture and art selected for the mansion by past governors and brought from China, England, France, Ireland, and Italy.

They made their way down the hallway stopping in the **Drawing Room**, with its beautiful fireplace and Steinway piano. The Waterford crystal chandelier that hung in the center of the room once hung in the White House when President Ulysses S. Grant helped the nation celebrate its centennial, or one-hundredth birthday. This was the same year, 1876, that Colorado became a state.

They walked, room by room, passing the library on the right and the circular stairs on the left, with the

Courtesy of Dottie Lamm

First Lady Dottie Lamm peeks at the portraits of former first ladies of Colorado that hang in the entrance hall of the Governor's Mansion.

State Dining Room just beyond. President Dwight D. Eisenhower, aviation pioneer Charles Lindbergh, and many Hollywood stars had dined in this stately room.

At the end of the hallway, Dottie and Heather entered the Palm Room with its white marble floors and high arched windows that overlooked the garden. Each window was **etched** with a different design. An **ornate** double fountain stood in the center of the rose garden. At the far end of the garden was a lovely old carriage house. Far beyond the garden, they could see Pikes Peak, seventy-five miles away, near Colorado Springs.

Every room was grandly decorated with paintings, lovely vases and lamps, carved wooden furniture, and interesting old carpets. The new governor's wife looked at the pictures of all the former governors and their families that hung in the Music Room. An inspiring group of people had led the State of Colorado for nearly one hundred years. No wonder Dottie felt apprehensive.

She saw that Scott and Heather were feeling some of the same concern that she was. If the governor felt a sense of awe, he didn't show it. He wore a huge smile and was eager to explore each new room. Dottie knew that their children needed her assurance that living in the mansion would be a wonderful adventure. She took a deep breath and smiled happily, too. This was a world away from the modest house on South Logan Street they had just left. Dottie realized the huge responsibility and many **adjustments** that this lifestyle would bring to all of them.

Fortunately, the former governor's wife, Ann Love, understood that the mansion was not suitable for a family with young children. She had created a home for the governors' families on the second and third floors and kept the first floor for official use.

Mrs. Love had opened the beautiful home for public tours. The Lamms decided to continue that tradition. They wanted the people of Colorado to see the elegant mansion, built by Walter Scott Cheesman in 1908. Cheesman died before it was completed. It was sold to Claude Boettcher, who used it as a private residence. Mr. Boettcher owned the American Crystal Sugar Company and other businesses. He gave the mansion to his wife as a Valentine's Day present in 1924. The Claude Boettcher estate donated the mansion to the State of Colorado in 1969.

The new first family continued their stroll through the twenty-seven rooms. The upstairs rooms where they would live were much more comfortable than the formal downstairs. Later that day, friends and family arrived with flowers and good wishes. It didn't take long for Heather and Scott to put their toys away in their own rooms. Now they began to feel at home.

2 New Friends

On the day Dottie and her family moved into the Governor's Mansion, she thought for a few moments back to her childhood. Most little girls dream of being a princess, wearing beautiful clothes, and being the belle of the ball. Dottie was no exception. And now, here she was, entering a fairytale life—or some people might think that was so.

Dottie was born in the Bronx, New York, on May 23, 1937, where her father, John K. Vennard, was a **civil engineering** professor at New York University. Living in a large city meant that when she played outdoors, she was watched very carefully by her parents and didn't have much freedom.

When Dottie was nine years old, her family moved across the country to Palo Alto, California. Her father had taken a teaching job at Stanford University. Moving wasn't easy. Her sister, Jane, was too young to care. When their father said, "Take one more look at the George Washington Bridge," Jane just said, "Good-bye, stupid." But Dottie remembers the ache in her throat and the tears that stung her cheeks as they drove away. She cried softly into her pillow that night in the motel.

Palo Alto was a lovely place, and she soon appreciated the freedom it allowed. She liked to ride her bike to the Stanford campus and sketch pictures. Although she wasn't a very good artist, she drew well enough for it to be an interesting hobby. She sat under the big oak and eucalyptus trees on the campus and sketched the things that swirled through her mind. Dottie enjoyed having quiet time alone. It gave her time to think about her new school and the classmates she hoped to meet.

Dottie was a little nervous about meeting new people. She hoped she could make enough friends to feel at home and to have a good time. After school started, and she began to make friends, one of the girls told her, "I just want you to know that everyone thinks you are becoming popular." Dottie was surprised and happy. After all, everyone wants to be liked by other people. Later, she realized that seeking popularity wasn't always the best thing. Sometimes it caused her to ask herself, "Will this make me popular? Will that make me popular?" She did have friends and had a good time with them. She learned that she didn't have to work at being popular.

The Vennard home was a happy and stable place for the two girls to grow up. Mrs. Vennard was a loving and supportive mother.

Dorothy Walton Vennard had been a junior high school math teacher before she married. During the

Dottie and her mother,
Dorothy Walton Vennard.

Depression, women seldom worked outside the home. Employers would not hire women if their husband had jobs. So, she turned her attention to taking care of her family and volunteering with the girls' activities.

Mrs. Vennard led her daughters' Brownie and Girl Scout troops. The girls also joined the Rainbow Girls, an organization that emphasized community service.

The family belonged to the First Congregational Church in Palo Alto, where Dottie's parents worked on church committees. Their church helped many people in the community, whether they were church members or not. Members believed that helping others was the most important work they could do. This was one of the main reasons that the Vennards chose this church.

Professor Vennard had been the first person in his family to attend college. As a young man, he worked hard to save enough money to go to college. He understood that his education had made it possible for him to provide for his family and have a comfortable home. Because Dottie's parents thought education was important, the girls were expected to do their best in school.

One time, Dottie came home with a low grade. Her parents said, "If we thought this was the best you could do, it would be acceptable. But we just don't believe you are trying hard enough. Always do your best work."

Not all of the male professors at the university accepted women as their equals in the teaching profession. This was especially true in the engineering school, but Professor Vennard was supportive of the women engineering professors and students. The other professors were happy to have him deal with them.

Professor Vennard had a sense of humor and loved puns. He had a quick wit, so suppertime usually included laughter. He drew the line when the humor turned into teasing. Dottie recalled once teasing her sister at the table. Jane got so angry that she threw a dinner roll at Dottie. Jane was sent from the table, and Dottie was scolded.

Dottie and her younger sister were three years apart in age, and they seldom played together. Dottie was social and loved to spend time with her friends. Jane thought of Dottie as "always on the go." On the other hand, Jane was serious and happy to be at home with her family. The only time they played together was on family trips when they did not have other friends around. Then, they spent hours playing Hearts. Both girls loved to read. Nancy Drew books were favorites. They also shared a love for their pet dog, Waggo, who was happy to play with either of the girls. Although they didn't spend a lot of time together and they often argued, Dottie always stood up for her younger sister if someone was unkind to her. She knew that standing up for her sister was important.

When the family left New York, Dottie and Jane's Grandmother Vennard moved with them. She was a

Know More!

Nancy Drew Series
Nancy Drew is a fictional character in an adventure mystery book series that has remained popular for several generations. The author's name on the books is Carolyn Keene. Carolyn Keene is a pen name for Mildred Wirt Benson who was hired in 1929 to write the first three books and who later wrote twenty more. At least ten other authors have written Nancy Drew books and published them under the name Carolyn Keene. If you were to choose a pen name, what would it be? Try writing the first paragraphs of a mystery. Include your main character's name and where and when the story takes place. Perhaps you will want to continue writing until you have completed a book.

widow and their only living grandparent. Grandmother Vennard was a professional **seamstress**, and she taught the girls to sew when they were in elementary school. By the time they were in junior high school, Dottie and Jane made most of their clothes.

Dottie loved to sew and loved stylish clothes. She and her friends had a sewing club they called The Ten Tiny Tinkers Sewing Club. But Dottie did not want the boys to think she was only interested in doing "girl stuff".

The boys teased the girls saying, "All the girls do is sit at home and sew—nah-nah, nah-nah, nah-nah."

The girls called back, "No, we don't. We play baseball and we go to scouts, just like you guys do. So, nah-nah to you, too."

Dottie would not let those boys tell her what she was interested in or could do.

Dottie and her friends once started a club called the Junior Police. They hoped to catch a neighborhood woman they thought was poisoning animals. The Junior Police sneaked around the woman's house looking for evidence. Dottie's parents learned what the boys and girls were doing and insisted that Dottie stop. Six months later, the woman was arrested by the real police for poisoning animals. How the Junior Police wished that they could have caught her, just as Nancy Drew would have done!

Dottie and her younger sister, Jane, dressed up for Easter in 1943

Courtesy of Dottie Lamm

Three-year-old Dottie with her grandmother, Mabel Walton, in her garden in Portsmouth, New Hampshire

Courtesy of Dottie Lamm

3 Growing Up

The Vennard family vacations usually involved outdoor activities. It was a short drive from their home in Palo Alto to the mountains of California, so they spent time there year round. They loved to hike and camp. They also skied frequently. When the girls were very young, Professor Vennard had made tiny wooden skis for them to practice on.

One of Dottie's favorite memories was of the time she and her father had skied at Badger Pass in Yosemite National Park. Professor Vennard kept making jokes. Dottie laughed so hard she fell off the rope tow!

Dottie and Jane's father taught them to target-shoot. No one in their family liked to hunt, but they enjoyed the sport of shooting at a target.

When Dottie was about twelve, she and her father went to a Stanford football game. Dottie had never

Courtesy of Dottie Lamm

*Jane and Dottie ready to ski at Badger Pass,
Yosemite National Park, California, in 1949.*

doubted that her father loved her, but she did have a question she had been wondering about.

Reluctantly, she asked her father, "Did you ever wish that either my sister or I had been a boy?"

"No," her father replied, "I don't think so. Name one thing a son could do that you girls can't,"

"Well, play football."

"This isn't a sport that really matters," he said. "It's individual skills or companionship sports, things that will last you all your life, that are important."

Dottie smiled and enjoyed the rest of the game.

Dottie and Jane grew up during World War II. There was a **shortage** of many items during the war. Gasoline was hard to get, so people did not take vacations very far from home. One time their family went on a camping trip with another family to Yosemite National Park in northern California. This trip was always a fond memory because they were able to ride on pack mules up the mountain.

Many times, the Vennards' holidays were shared with students from foreign countries or with those who, for other reasons, could not go home to be with their families. Christmas celebrations were more about sharing with others than about gifts received. Dottie's father had grown up in a family that had very little money. The girls were taught early that those from poor backgrounds should be treated with respect and justice.

In high school, Dottie learned her first political lesson. In her senior year, she ran for commissioner of girls' activities. She had been junior class secretary and a cheerleader, and because she was quite popular, her friends encouraged her to run for commissioner. She lost the election and was terribly disappointed. Later, she realized that the girl who won was much better qualified for the job. Dottie would not have liked to do all that was expected of the position. She learned to choose activities that she was really interested in and willing to do.

Another valuable lesson Dottie learned was to follow her own instincts and good judgment. It was easy to put too much emphasis on being popular. Adults in her life helped her see that it was important to think for herself rather than to listen to others.

The minister of the First Congregational Church of Palo Alto, Reverend Arthur Casaday influenced Dottie very much. Reverend Casady was confined to a wheelchair. Before he was **paralyzed** by polio, he had been a football player and athlete. He impressed her with his kindness and with his commitment to help others.

Dottie's high school English teacher, Craig Vittetoe, brought out the best work in his students. He was such a good teacher that Dottie thought he "even made grammar come alive." Grammar would be important to her later when she began to write a newspaper column.

Dottie had two heroines she had never met. One was Eleanor Roosevelt, wife of President Franklin D. Roosevelt, a very important lady in her own right. Another was Amelia Earhart, a pioneering pilot during the early years of aviation. Earhart was the first woman to fly solo across both the Atlantic Ocean and from Hawaii to California in the Pacific Ocean. She encouraged other women to follow their own interests and to take risks.

Dottie and Jane always knew they would go to college. Dottie later recalled, "My father was ahead of his time in that he didn't object to my having a career. But he did believe the main goal of a college education for a woman was to prepare her to be an enlightened wife and mother. Dad also thought that with a college education a woman would know how to better take care of herself and her children if she were on her own.

For many young women in the 1950s and 1960s being an enlightened, self sufficient wife and mother

Know More!

Eleanor Roosevelt

Eleanor Roosevelt, wife of President Franklin D. Roosevelt, was one of the most admired women in America for many years. She helped change child labor laws to prevent children from working long hours in factories. She also felt that African-American children in the South should go to school with white children.

During the Depression, when many people were out of jobs, she started camps to teach women new skills and traveled across the country to see for herself the problems of unemployed people. Mrs. Roosevelt often spoke on the radio, and in her daily newspaper column she often wrote about **underprivileged** people who could not always speak for themselves. Later, she became a delegate from the United States to the United Nations. In what ways were Eleanor Roosevelt and Dottie Lamm alike?

Write a newspaper column explaining why African-American children should have been allowed to go to school with white children.

was not reason enough to go to college. Like other girls, Dottie wanted to have a career, as well as be a mother and a volunteer. Later, as a newspaper columnist, she would write about the struggles women faced as they balanced family life and careers.

In 1955, Dottie enrolled at Occidental College in California. She had always been interested in how the human mind works. This interest led her to study psychology. During summer vacations, she worked on an assembly line at a computer factory. The job was boring and she disliked it, but it helped her realize that a good education was necessary for a good job. Dottie graduated with honors in 1959 and could now think about a career.

4 Flying into a New Life

Shortly after graduation, Dottie found the job that would take her places. She became an airline **stewardess** for United Airlines. Today, airline stewardesses are called flight attendants. Her warm personality and ready smile made people feel welcome when they stepped onboard the plane. When Dottie completed her training in Cheyenne, Wyoming, she chose Denver, Colorado as her "home base."

At Christmastime in 1961, Dottie and her roommate had a party. One of the guests asked if she could bring two friends to the party. One of them was Dick Lamm, a young lawyer who had recently moved to Denver. Although too many guests had already been invited, Dottie agreed that it would be okay. Not long after the party, Dick called Dottie for a date. She turned him down, because she couldn't remember

Courtesy of Dottie Lamm

In the 1960s, when Dottie worked as a stewardess for United Airlines, the uniform included hat, gloves, and pumps.

him, and anyway, she was too tired. In January, he called again. This time she reluctantly accepted a date. They discovered they shared many interests and continued dating. Two years later, on May 11, 1963, Dottie and Dick were married in the First Unitarian Church of Denver, Colorado.

In the 1960s, the airlines did not allow married women to work as stewardesses. Dottie gave up flying and got a job as a case worker at the Denver Department of Welfare. Soon, she began working on a master's degree in **psychiatric social work** at the University of Denver. She had always had a desire to do something that would help less-fortunate people. A master's degree would give her the education she needed to fulfill that goal.

At the same time, her new husband was running for the Colorado House of Representatives. Dottie campaigned for him by going door-to-door and talking to people about Dick and explaining why he would be a good **legislator**. All the hard work paid off. Dick Lamm was elected to the House in 1966.

Dottie's own interest in politics began to grow. In the 1960s, the South was in the middle of turmoil. Dr. Martin Luther King Jr. led people to support equal rights for black people. Long before this, in 1870, black

Courtesy of Dottie Lamm

Dottie and Dick on their wedding day, May 11, 1963.

men had been given the right to vote in the 15th Amendment to the United States Constitution.

One of the reasons many of them were unable to vote was because they were not registered. Some states kept black people from registering by requiring a literacy test. Other states denied voting rights to poor blacks by requiring citizens to pay a poll tax before they could vote.

Know More!

Dr. Martin Luther King Jr.
Martin Luther King Jr. grew up in Georgia where he attended segregated schools. He graduated from high school when he was fifteen years old. He graduated from Morehouse College, then went to Crozer Theological Seminary in Pennsylvania to study to be a pastor, like his father and grandfather. At Boston University he completed his doctorate degree and met and married Coretta Scott. They had two daughters and two sons.

Dr. King was a minister, an author, and an inspiring civil rights leader who traveled more than six million miles to speak in places where people were being treated unfairly. He called upon his followers to use peaceful means to call attention to discrimination and change laws. King was respected around the world. His "I Have a Dream" speech is one of the most famous and important speeches ever given. Dr. King was the youngest man to win a world-famous prize. Can you find out the name of the prize? Hint: It had to do with his peaceful ways. What did he do with the $54,123 prize money?

People came from all over the country to march with Dr. King and to help black people register to vote. In 1965, Dottie went with other activists from Denver to Selma, Alabama, to join the march in support of Dr. King. She knew it was the right thing to do. Sometimes people grew angry at these **demonstrations** and turned to violence against those who were supporting Dr. King and his cause. Dr. King encouraged everyone to stay calm. Dottie later said she was glad she was able to support black people in this important cause for their freedom.

The 1960s were a busy time for Dottie. She completed her master's degree in 1967 from the University of Denver and earned the Sinnock Award for outstanding graduate in the School of Social Work. And, on December 19, 1967, Scott Hunter Lamm was born to his proud parents.

Dottie was working at this time for the University of Colorado Health Sciences Center. Her work with people who had very big problems and very little money influenced her thinking and her future career. She felt that most of these people could not help the situations they were in, and yet they were not respected by many people. Her next job was at the Florence Crittenden Home, working with unmarried pregnant women and their families. Both jobs helped her understand what needy families are like and how to help them.

She became aware that even the professionals she worked with often did not understand her clients and their circumstances. She was disappointed when a male social worker said, "I don't see why women need equal pay. Most don't have to work, and their husbands support them anyway."

This was especially upsetting because he said it in front of a widow who was raising two teenagers alone. Dottie was surprised and annoyed by her co-worker's attitude. He worked with single mothers often and should have known how difficult it was for them to care for their families.

Dottie held her temper as she turned and walked away, but she knew his attitude was unfair. She began to think about what she could do to change people's minds and to create fair laws. She was determined to try to influence others. The next week, she joined the National Organization for Women to support laws that would do away with discrimination against women. Equal Pay for Equal Work was their motto.

Dick Lamm ran again for the Colorado House of Representatives in 1968. Dottie again campaigned for her husband. This time, she put young Scott in a backpack and headed out to meet people. She worked tirelessly with her husband, and they were successful in getting him reelected.

In 1970, when the Lamms welcomed their second child, Heather Elizabeth, Dottie decided to leave her job and stay home with her two young children. She kept busy taking care of them and helping her husband.

Dottie never lost her love of outdoor activities, such as running. She and her husband liked to run

Courtesy of Dottie Lamm

*In 1968, Dottie campaigned for Dick with baby
Scott in a backpack.*

Courtesy of Dottie Lamm

*When Dick ran for governor in 1973, Scott was six
and Heather was three.*

and compete in races. As a family, they hiked, skied, and climbed mountains. She was a role model for women, encouraging them to exercise for better health.

In 1973 Dick Lamm entered the race for governor of Colorado. Dottie knew this campaigning would be a big job and take a lot of time and energy. She hired someone to help care for their children and devoted more time to his campaign for governor. During the campaign, Dick Lamm walked 888 miles around the state—about the same distance as walking from Denver, Colorado, to Minneapolis, Minnesota. Whenever time would allow, Dottie walked around the state with him, meeting people and asking for their votes.

The Lamms spent all that year and the next campaigning, and in November 1974, Richard Lamm was elected governor of Colorado. They sold their modest home in Denver and moved into the Governor's Mansion in January 1975.

5 Colorado's First Family

In her role as wife of the governor, Dottie had many responsibilities, but her family came first. Both Governor and Mrs. Lamm arranged their schedules to spend time with their children. Governor Lamm was asked to speak at many dinners and to be present at receptions. Instead of spending the entire evening at these events, he would go home and play with the children, then go and give his speech after the dinner. Or he would go early, speak, and then return home for his own dinner. Dottie arranged her schedule to include the children. The family continued to enjoy frequent weekend camping and skiing trips.

While he was campaigning, Dick Lamm had stayed with people all across the state, in simple homes and large ones, in small towns and on huge ranches. He wanted to repay them for their kindness. He promised

Photo by Rocky Mountain News photographer G. Wilkinson

*Perhaps the Governor's Mansion is not the best place
for a Kool Aid stand. Scott and Heather wait
patiently for business.*

that if he were elected, they would be invited to a party right after the **inauguration**. Well, he was elected, and the Lamms did invite all those people, rich and poor, to come to a party. Now, they faced two problems. The Lamms had not hired a staff of workers yet, so they worried about how to prepare for this big group. And, no one in this group would know each other!

Just as the guests were to arrive, four-year-old Heather and the babysitter's daughter, Nikki Norton, disappeared. The partygoers had a real surprise when they arrived to find two little girls splashing in the beautiful fountain in the Palm Room! Two wet little girls were quickly taken upstairs to change clothes. It did make the guests laugh, though, so now everyone was more relaxed at the party.

Another time, Scott and Heather's pet hamster got loose and disappeared in the huge mansion for days. That's a lot of space for a hamster to explore. At least it didn't turn up at a formal reception! Their loving basset hound, Travis, was turned away from more than one reception. Travis discovered that dogs and formal occasions in a mansion do not go together!

The children agreed there were advantages to living in such a large residence. The basement was big enough for them to roller skate in it. It was as if they had a roller rink all to themselves. As a teenager, Scott belonged to a rock band that used the basement for practice sessions. Because the loud music could be heard throughout the house, his parents decided it was best that the band not practice on Tuesdays when the public tours were held.

Most of the twelve years that the Lamms lived in the Governor's Mansion, Scott and Heather went to public schools. Governor and Mrs. Lamm were pleased that their children made friends with children of all backgrounds.

Growing up in the Governor's Mansion had many advantages. But, at times it was difficult for Scott and Heather. People were always interested in the governor's family, so the newspapers reported just about everything the family did. When their names appeared in the paper, Heather and Scott were teased by classmates, and they were embarrassed. Scott was shy when he was young. It wasn't much fun for him to have his picture in the papers.

The Lamm parents had to remind their children that they were not wealthy. The spacious mansion that they were privileged to call home belonged to the people of Colorado.

6 Dottie Speaks Out

Dottie felt it was a **privilege** to be the first lady of Colorado. She also knew it was an opportunity to speak about the issues that concerned her. She led the Governor's Task Force on Children in 1976 and 1977. She was also a member of the Colorado Commission on Women. These groups studied social issues that affected women and children and made recommendations to improve the lives of women and children through educational opportunities, expanded health care benefits for children, and equal pay for women.

Dottie and her husband worked as partners. They were concerned with many of the same problems, such as the environment and how to keep their beautiful state from becoming polluted. They were also concerned about women's issues. Many women were working at

A Halloween party at the mansion in 1980 raised awareness of the
March of Dimes Crippled Children Campaign.

Courtesy of Dottie Lamm

important jobs, yet they were not paid the same as a man doing the same work. Dottie often spoke to groups about the governor's ideas and policies.

The Lamms also were concerned about the people that Dottie had seen in her job as a social worker. Many of them had large families and continued to have more children, even though they were unable to care for them. Dottie had met many single parents, usually women, who could not meet the financial

Santa Claus and the First Lady entertained children from the local Head Start program in 1978.

needs of their families, no matter how hard they tried. Thus, she worked tirelessly for them to have the right to plan and control their family size. Years later, she wrote about her concerns in her weekly *Denver Post* column. One of her readers said, "Dottie has a heart that cares about others, and she is willing to do something about it."

In 1976, America celebrated its 200th birthday, or its **bicentennial**, and Colorado celebrated its **centennial**, or 100th birthday. At the same time, an Equal Rights Amendment to the U.S. Constitution was being discussed and considered by lawmakers.

Women were granted the right to vote when the Nineteenth Amendment to the Constitution was passed, but men still had rights that women were not permitted. The Equal Rights Amendment, which would have been the twenty-seventh Amendment, was proposed in 1972. Thirty-eight of the fifty states needed to approve it before it could become an Amendment. Only thirty-five states voted for it. Colorado was one of the many states that approved its own state Equal Rights Amendments.

However, some groups were trying to take away, or rescind, these laws. It was important to Dottie to see that women had equal rights to men. Many women

Know More!

Women's Movement

Although the women's rights movement wasn't recognized until 1848, strong women like Abigail Adams did much for women much earlier. Abigail was the wife of the second U.S. president, John Adams, and the mother of the fifth president, John Quincy Adams. In 1776, Abigail wrote a letter to her husband, saying, "In the new code of laws, remember the ladies and do not put such unlimited powers into the hands of the husbands." She also encouraged her husband to support education for women and to oppose slavery.

Other women who were important in getting equal rights for women were Susan B. Anthony, Lucretia Mott, and Elizabeth Cady Stanton. Later Eleanor Roosevelt, Gloria Steinem, and others continued the work. Choose one of these notable women and find out what she did to support rights for women. Design a postage stamp honoring one of the leaders in gaining women's rights.

Which amendment to the U.S. Constitution gave women the right to vote? In what year were women granted the right to vote?

she knew were stay-at-home mothers, but that was not the case for all women. She could not understand why a woman would not be paid the same salary for doing the same job. Women should be given equal rights with men. They could choose how they would use these rights, whether in the workplace or at home. The 1977 Nobel Prize winner for medicine, Rosalyn Yalow, said, "The world cannot afford the loss of talents of half of its people if we are to solve the many problems which beset us." Women were needed in jobs where their skills could be used to solve problems. Dottie was committed to making these things happen.

During this year of celebration, Dottie wanted to call attention to the good things about her state. She invited 63 members of the Colorado Commission on Women to climb the 14,110-foot Pikes Peak, near Colorado Springs. The women hiked to honor Katherine Lee Bates who wrote "America, the Beautiful" while she was a visiting professor at Colorado College in Colorado Springs. Bates went to the top of Pikes Peak in a horse-drawn prairie wagon. The amazing view from the top of the mountain inspired her to write the words to the much-loved song.

On the day the commission members climbed the mountain, one lady came in high heels! Fortunately, someone loaned her a pair of sneakers. After a hard climb to the mountain top, the women placed a scroll with the climbers' names and a proclamation from the governor honoring Bates.

Dottie had kept a journal from the time that Dick Lamm first ran for office. She wrote about the events they shared and the concerns they had over the years. Dottie used her journal to begin a column for the *Denver Post.* She hoped that her experience and her position as first lady would encourage people to think about the problems facing the state.

Her first column appeared in February 1979. She wrote articles about problems that families had, that single parents faced, and about concerns of **disadvantaged** people, especially children. Dottie wanted her readers to understand that there needed to be a balance between the independence women sought and their desire to work as equal partners with men. Her honest opinions encouraged women of all backgrounds. Her column was an instant success, and she became a strong voice for women's issues during the seventeen years she wrote for the *Denver Post.*

Governor Lamm was reelected in 1978 and again in 1982. Because an economic slump had left many people out of work, the Lamms did not hold a traditional Inauguration Ball in 1982. Instead, they requested that the money that would have been donated by the public for the party go either to the Salvation Army or to Care and Share to benefit the less-fortunate people of Colorado.

While living in the Governor's Mansion, the Lamms had little privacy. They entertained at both large and small events, hosting **official** dignitaries, Hollywood celebrities, and held many charity events, including formal dinners, recitals, and dances. But, the elegant house the Lamms lived in was old and needed frequent repairs. People were often in the mansion to make repairs. It seemed to the family that repairmen showed up in their big house all the time. Having people in and out of their home was only one of the new things that Dottie, Dick, Heather, and Scott had to learn to adjust to during their years in the mansion.

Know More!

Katherine Lee Bates

In 1893, Katherine Lee Bates wrote the words to the much-loved hymn "America, the Beautiful" after a visit by horse and wagon to the top of Pikes Peak. She was so inspired by the view from the top of the mountain that, when she returned to Colorado Springs, she wrote the poem. Where and when was Katherine L. Bates born? Who composed the music for the poem? Write a poem or a letter to a friend describing a beautiful place you have been.

7 Unexpected Challenge

In 1981, Dottie was faced with her greatest challenge yet. She had always been concerned with others' problems, but now she had her own. On Labor Day 1981, Dottie was **diagnosed** with breast cancer. Her children were thirteen and ten years old, and Governor Lamm was in his seventh year as governor. Many hard decisions had to be made about the best way to fight the disease, but Dottie's first priority was to be strong in spirit for her family. Because she was a public figure, she also had to think of the best way to tell the people of Colorado about what she was facing. She decided not to keep the news a secret or else the public might think she could not be cured. So, she had an announcement made right away.

A difficult year began because the **treatment** for breast cancer would take many months. She reassured her family that she would be all right. She did not want to worry her husband, as he needed to concentrate on his job. Dottie had surgery in September 1981 and started **chemotherapy** that would continue for a year.

Dottie often wrote poetry when she felt discouraged. During her illness, writing poetry helped her feel hopeful. While she was ill, she continued to write her column and let others know about her progress. Other famous people were helpful and encouraging. Happy Rockefeller, wife of Governor Nelson Rockefeller of New York, had survived breast cancer. Former President Gerald Ford's wife, Betty, had also had breast cancer and made a trip to Denver to see Dottie. People from all over the country wrote to her. Their letters helped her keep her courage and determination to do everything she needed to do to get well.

Dottie researched breast cancer and its treatments. She learned to eat foods that would give her more strength, and she gave up foods that were not good for her. She sought **spiritual** growth by reading books on religion and spirituality. She focused on personal goals such as seeing her children grow up and being at her daughter's wedding. Dottie thought about the words of Louisa May Alcott, author of *Little Women,* who said, "I'm not afraid of the storm for I can steer my own boat." Dottie used everything she had learned that would help her "steer the boat", so she would be well once again.

During the time she was recovering from the surgery, Dottie returned to her mother's home in California. She relaxed in the warm sunshine and became certain that she would fully recover. She wrote letters to other breast cancer patients to encourage them.

Dottie also had time to think about her own loving family. What a blessing it was when ten-year-old Heather learned of her illness and asked, "You're going into the hospital? Who will take me on my back-to-school shopping trip?" Then Heather asked the more serious question, "Mom, are you going to die?" Dottie was glad she could talk to Heather about what she was really afraid of.

Her teenage son, Scott, loved to ride his bicycle and be with his friends. But one beautiful fall Saturday while Dottie was recovering, he and a friend stayed indoors in the small, hot kitchen and baked poppy seed bread to surprise his mother. "Mom, we just wanted to do something for you," he said.

All the time, her devoted husband did his own research. He called medical centers across the country to be sure Dottie was getting the best treatment. And her sister, now her special friend, was keeping their family and friends informed about how Dottie was feeling.

Dottie thought about things her mother had said to her over the years. Her mother often said, "You and your sister are individuals. You don't have to be just alike."

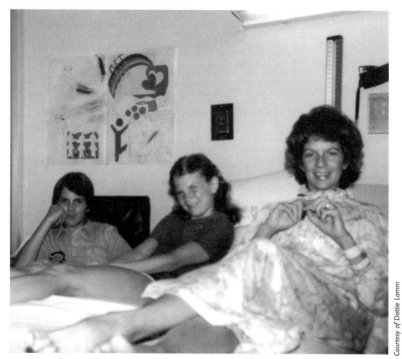

Dottie enjoyed a visit from her family while recovering from breast cancer surgery in September 1981.

Courtesy of Dottie Lamm

"Thank you, Mother, for saying that," thought Dottie.

"Of course you can have a baby and have a career also," her mother had said, even though she and her own mother lived in a time when middle class women usually had to choose between a family and a job.

"Thank you, Mother, for saying that," thought Dottie. She felt her family's love, and set about getting well.

"Readers had encouraged me to put my columns in book form. In 1982, while I was recuperating from cancer, I was moved to take their advice." Dottie selected articles she had written for the *Denver Post* and combined them in a book she titled *Second Banana*.

"This is a book about relationships between women and men, child to parent, friend to friend, and an individual to our society and to his or her God," she said.

Dottie recalled, "In my first column in 1979, I wrote that I had always dreamed of a professional way I could put my political, social work, homemaker and motherhood experiences to work all at once. This book is that arena."

Dottie became grateful for each new day and her return to good health. During this time, she decided on yet another way she could help women. She used her own experience with cancer to encourage women to have regular **mammograms**, an X-ray that can detect breast cancer. Further, she wanted to show women they could have full professional and personal lives after surviving cancer surgery. Dottie resumed her own busy schedule and finished the many important tasks she had begun before she became ill.

8 World Delegate

Following her year of treatment, Dottie directed her focus and energy toward helping people who were unlikely to be able to speak for themselves. She continued to write on topics that affected them, such as finances, family size, and health care. She wanted policies and new laws that would help them take care of themselves and their families.

In 1986, she and other concerned women started the Women's Foundation of Colorado with the mission to improve the lives of women and girls throughout the state. Dottie became the organization's first president.

Since Dottie worked countless hours for the Women's Foundation and because she was a respected community leader, the foundation created an award to honor her commitment to the women and girls of Colorado. The Dottie Lamm Award is given each year to high school sophomore girls who demonstrate "service and compassionate values." This **scholarship** is given to encourage the girls to become good leaders and role models. Girls are assigned to work with community leaders to learn how to become leaders themselves. These girls then help train younger girls. This way, there will always be new girls who receive leadership training.

Meanwhile, Governor Lamm had been elected to a third term in 1982. He continued to serve until 1986. The year after leaving office, Dick Lamm was invited to be a guest professor at Dartmouth College in Hanover, New Hampshire. By this time, Scott had left home for college and Heather accompanied her parents for a semester at Hanover High School. The Lamms returned to Dartmouth in 1995. This time they held a Joint Montgomery Fellowship, which meant they would teach together. They taught courses on population growth and other world problems.

They had enjoyed teaching together, but they returned to Colorado where, they agreed, "their hearts were."

Dick Lamm began teaching at the University of Denver's School of Public Policy. Dottie worked to find new ways to solve problems related to families.

She volunteered much time for the Women's Foundation of Colorado and the Centre for Development and Population Activities. She had grown up in a time when women's duties at home required most of their time. With timesaving appliances and with husbands sharing more of the household tasks, it was no longer necessary for women to be homemakers only. Now, the "other half of our population" could work in jobs that, traditionally, had been closed to women. Dottie wanted this to be a positive change and to see women use their skills and work as partners with men. She spoke to groups, appeared on television, and wrote articles on health issues and equality for women.

Dottie continued to be an outdoor enthusiast. She used her interest in the outdoors to support laws that would ensure clean air and water. Dottie's early years of mountain climbing with her family kept nudging her to climb again. By 1997, she had climbed 35 of Colorado's Fourteeners, the mountains that are higher than 14,000 feet.

Dottie had earned the respect of national leaders. President Bill Clinton appointed her to be an official delegate to the United Nations Conference on Population and Development in Cairo, Egypt, in 1994. A year later, she attended the Fourth World Conference

Throughout her life, Dottie has participated in sports.

Courtesy of Dottie Lamm

Know More!

Fourteeners
Dottie Lamm has climbed thirty-five Colorado mountains that are 14,000 feet or more above sea level. These are known as "Fourteeners." There is less oxygen in the air this high, so breathing is more difficult. Climbers must be in good health. How many fourteeners are there in Colorado? Does any other state have more? How many miles high would you be at the top of a "Fourteener"? Draw a picture of the view from the top of a fourteener. You may want to try chalk, water color paints, crayons or markers.

on Women in Bejing, China. Women from all over the world attended to gain a better understanding of the problems they faced and to hear new ideas for solving them. A highlight of this conference was a speech by Hillary Clinton. Ms. Clinton said, "Human rights are women's rights."

One purpose of the women's conference was to bring women together to plan how to make the lives of all children better. Sometimes they didn't agree about how children should be raised. They did agree that, "In all actions concerning children, the best interest of the child shall be a primary consideration."

These world conferences helped Dottie understand more about topics that had been important to her

Courtesy of the White House

Former first lady of Colorado with First Lady Hillary Clinton at a White House reception for the delegates to the Fourth World Conference on Women held in Bejing, China.

most of her life. Her interest in the problems of developing nations began years earlier on visits to India and Latin American countries, where she saw hungry and sick children. By attending the conferences, she was able to bring new information back to her own country with ideas on how to put this new information to work.

9 Setback and Victory

In 1998 Dottie ran for the United States Senate. She had a "vision of a better fiscal, educational, and environmental world for Colorado's children and grandchildren." She felt new leadership was needed to be sure the country's money was being spent for the important issues of education and health care. Dottie also felt that better laws had to be made to protect the environment.

Dottie was disappointed when she was defeated by the **incumbent** senator, Ben Nighthorse Campbell, but her dedication to helping less-fortunate women and children was not defeated. She once again turned her energy into work that she felt would do the most good by writing about possible solutions to their problems.

Dottie compiled her *Denver Post* articles from 1980 to 1996 into a second book, *Choice Concerns.*

Courtesy of Dottie Lamm

When Dottie decided to run for the senate in 1998, Heather was eager to help with the campaign.

Although many of the problems she had written about over the years were improving, some remained the same. While women were able to hold more types of jobs, they were often unable to get the top positions with a company or in politics. Because of this, Dottie began to work with two groups: Women Helping Women and The White House Project which encouraged young women to enter politics by giving them money and help with their campaigns.

Dottie continued her work with **overpopulation** through the Centre for Development and Population

Activities. She had kept in mind the extremely poor people she had seen years before in India. Dottie brought her valuable experiences from the two international conferences to this organization that worked with women in Asia, Latin America, and the United States. Dottie also met with world leaders to ask their support for continued progress in family planning for poor nations.

The Centre for Development and Population Activities and some other organizations began to understand how they could help poor people work their way out of poverty. The women in poor countries made beautiful crafts, but they did not have the money to start businesses for selling their handiwork. Banks were not used to working with women and refused to loan money to them. International development organizations began programs that convinced banks to make low-cost loans to women. Women were then able to start their businesses and could pay back the loans. Things began to happen! Now poor women had a way to make money and provide for their families.

On a return visit to Pakistan and India, Dottie could see the success the women had now that they had the money and support to start small businesses. Dottie thought, "Yes, if women have the power to change things for their families, they will do so. Empowering women to make decisions and to establish businesses is a way to provide for their families."

When the women came together to establish companies, they were given the opportunity to learn about family planning, education for their children, and good nutrition. Dottie began to feel hopeful that families would not have more children than they could provide for. She told her fellow workers, "We are seeing the progress. We must continue the fight."

Know More!

Dottie Lamm takes her motto for life from American singer Kate Smith who said, "Find out what you care about and live a life that shows it."

What is a motto? How does it differ from a slogan? Choose or write a motto for your own life.

10 Grandmother and Grand Lady

In 1999, Dottie was named Leo Block Professor and taught courses on population and leadership issues at the University of Denver. She spoke throughout the country on risk taking and leadership. She also spoke on the topic, "Living with Success and Failure." Dottie knew this subject well because she had discovered how to turn failure into success.

From 2003 to 2005, Dottie returned to teach at the Graduate School of Social Work at the University of Denver, where she once had been a student. Drawing on years of experience, she helped students better understand the problems of disadvantaged people.

This creative, accomplished leader among women is much admired because of her caring nature and because she uses her abilities to help people, regardless of race, religion, or gender. She has been honored by

Grandbabies fill Dottie's life and heart. Scott's son, Kennon, was born in 2006 joining his cousin, Jasper, born to Heather in 2004.

numerous organizations all over the United States for her many accomplishments.

Her honors and awards include:

- Women's Foundation of Colorado's Dottie Lamm Scholarship
- B'nai B'rith Community Service Award
- Colorado Black Women for Political Action Appreciation Award
- Colorado Women's Hall of Fame
- Mental Health Association Tribute
- Anti-Defamation League's Civil Rights Award
- Big Sisters of Colorado Contributions Award
- 1967 Outstanding Graduate, University of Denver's Social Work Sinnock Award
- The Occidental College Gold Seal Alumni Award for Public Service

Dottie Lamm continues the work that has been important to her throughout her life. She remains an advocate for population planning and is always ready to lend her advice and experience to organizations that help women succeed.

Dottie Lamm's many roles have included home-maker, political wife, published author, social worker, politician, **feminist**, lecturer, teacher, cancer survivor,

outdoor enthusiast, concerned citizen, and now grandmother who inspires future generations. Dottie Lamm
has not only learned the formula for success, but she
continues to share it with others.

Courtesy of Dottie Lamm

Timeline

May 23, 1937 – Born in Bronx, New York

1946 – Moves to Palo Alto, California

1959 – Graduates from Occidental College

1959 – Begins job as United Airlines stewardess

May 11, 1963 – Marries Dick Lamm at First Unitarian Church, Denver, Colorado

1965 – Marches with Martin Luther King Jr. in Selma, Alabama

1966 – Campaigns door-to-door for Dick Lamm for House of Representatives

1967 – Receives the Sinnock Award for outstanding graduate at the University of Denver Graduate School of Social Work

1967 – Son Scott Hunter Lamm born

1970 – Daughter Heather Elizabeth Lamm born

1974 – Campaigns for Dick Lamm for Colorado Governor

January 1975 – Moves into the Governor's Mansion as First Lady of Colorado

1978 – Campaigns for her husband's reelection bid

February 1979 – First *Denver Post* column appears

September 1981 – Diagnosis of breast cancer, surgery, and chemotherapy

1982 – Governor Dick Lamm elected for a third term

1994 – Appointed by President Bill Clinton as delegate to U.N. Conference on Population and Development in Cairo, Egypt

1995 – Teaches at Dartmouth University in a joint Montgomery Fellowship with Dick Lamm

Delegate to Fourth World Conference on Women in Bejing, China

1997 – Unsuccessful campaign for U.S. Senate

1999 – Named Leo Block Professor at University of Denver

National and International keynote speaker and workshop leader

2003 – 2005 – Assistant clinical professor, Graduate School of Social Work, University of Denver

2004 – Grandson Jasper Lamm Ooms born

2006 – Grandson Kennon Hunter Lamm born

2007 – Grandson Tobias Vennard Ooms born

New Words

adjustment – action of setting right

apprehension – uneasy expectation

awe – wonder, respect

bicentennial – 200th anniversary

centennial – 100th anniversary

chemotherapy – medical treatment for cancer

civil engineer – expert in constructing engines

demonstrations – public expression of feelings for or against something through meetings, marches, etc.

diagnosed – to determine the nature of a disease

disadvantaged – economically or physically deprived

drawing room – formal room where guests are received

etch – to cut or engrave designs on glass

feminist – advocate of political, economic and social equality for women

inauguration – formally install in office

incumbent – holder of an office

influence – power used to sway a person; not by force

legislator – someone who is elected to make laws

mammograms – x-rays used to detect breast cancer

official – someone who holds public office

ornate – highly decorated

overpopulation – more people than the environment can sustain

paralyzed – inability to move a muscle or group of muscles

privilege – an advantage to one person or group

psychiatric social work – a profession that assists mental health patients

reluctant – hesitant to act

scholarship – financial award for someone to pursue studies

seamstress – a person who makes a living by sewing

shortage – less of something than is needed

spiritual – related to sacred or religious matters

stewardess – airline hostess; flight attendant

treatment – method of medical care

underprivileged – living below an acceptable level of social or economic conditions

Sources

Books

Lamm, Dottie. *Second Banana*. Boulder, CO: Johnson Books, 1983.

Lamm, Dottie. *Choice Concerns*. Privately printed, 1998.

Varnell, Jeanne. *Women of Consequence*. Boulder, CO: Johnson Books, 1999.

Interviews by Author

Dorothy Louise Vennard Lamm, May 4 and August 23, 2006.

Reverend Jane E. Vennard, June 29, 2006.

Newspaper Articles

Flynn, Kevin, "Politics Comes Naturally to Lamm," *Rocky Mountain News*, July 12, 1998.

Green, Chuck, "This Wild Hare Just May Run," *Denver Post*, July 13, 1997, p. B1.

Hartman, Diane, "Who Is This Woman? Dottie Lamm," *Denver Post*, October 23, 1997.

Lamm, Dottie, weekly columns, 1979-1986, *Denver Post*.

Lamm, Dottie, "Second Banana – Not Quite Equal Yet," *The Pen Woman* (L) Denver Branch, February, 2006.

Nyberg, Bartell, "Dottie Lamm...A Lot of Human Being," *Denver Post Empire Magazine*, February 14, 1982, p. 14.

Savage, Ania, "'Second Banana – No Slip for First Lady," *Rocky Mountain News*, October 1, 1983.

Web Sites

Biography of Dr. M. L. King. Official website of the Nobel Foundation. *http://nobelprize.org/nobel_prizes/peace/laureates/1964/index.html.*

Biography of Eleanor Roosevelt, *http://www.whitehouse.gov/history/firstladies/ar32.html*

"Colorado Fourteeners," *www.14ers.com*

Centre For Development and Population Activities. *www.cedpa.org*

Dottie Lamm Award. The Women's Foundation of Colorado, *www.wfco.org*

Eleanor Roosevelt. *en.wikipedia.org/wikiEleanor_Roosevelt*

"Eleanor Roosevelt." Doris Kearns Goodwin. *www.time.com/time/time100leaders/profile/eleanor.html*

"Governor's Residence at the Boettcher Mansion." *www.colorado.gov/governor/mansion/history.html*

Lamm, Dick and Dottie, "10 Commandments of Community." *www.rmpbs.org*, October 27, 2001

Lamm, Dottie, "Building the Future Takes Effort and Vision." *http://www.womenof.com/articles/ai030498.asp*, 1997.

Nancy Drew. *en-wikipedia-org/wiki/Nancy Drew*

"Non-partisan organization shaping U.S. policy to benefit poor women worldwide." Women's Edge Coalition. *www.womensedge.org*

"Women's Rights Movement." National Women's History Project. *http://www.nwhp.org/resourcecenter/linkswomensrights.php.*

Index

Acknowledgments

This book was written through the encouragement of publishers Doris and Tom Baker. Their enthusiasm for having Dottie Lamm's continuing story told and allowing me to write this story is much appreciated.

My special thanks goes to the staff of the Stephen H. Hart Library at the Colorado State Historical Society. I value their knowledge and their ever-ready assistance. I also appreciate the staff at The Denver Public Library, Special Collections, Western History/Genealogy Department. Each staff member was most helpful.

My granddaughter, Kaitlyn Warner, a fourth-grade student in State College, Pennsylvania, shared insightful questions for an interview with Dottie Lamm.

Thanks to my husband, Bud, who provided good questions.

My appreciation goes to Jeanne Nott Ellis, executive secretary to Richard Lamm, for providing biographical information.

Editor Kathleen Phillips contributed beneficial guidance and good suggestions to refine my ideas.

I thank Reverend Jane E. Vennard for her valuable time and her candid interview that provided a glimpse into her sister's life.

Above all others, thanks to Dottie Lamm for her ongoing support and cooperation with this project. She was always gracious and available for interviews or to answer questions. Dottie also spent hours collecting pictures and sharing those family treasures. Her openness has made writing her story a true pleasure.

About the Author

Emily B. Warner was drawn to writing Dottie Lamm's story through her love of biographies and her admiration for Dottie's work on behalf of disadvantaged families. Emily, a retired classroom teacher and teacher of gifted education, taught in nine states and in Italy. She lives in Colorado Springs, Colorado, with her husband. They have three grown sons and six grandchilren.